Hello I am Amaya. I can be found on 'X' and Instagram @youngmarinehero

I am 9 years old and have Autism, I struggle with the world around me. I am home schooled as I couldn't cope with the school environment. I have a support dog named Boo. She helps me to be able to cope in the world.

I am very passionate about marine life and want to be a marine biologist when I grow up. I go on beach clean ups most days. So I see what people leave and do to sea creatures e.g. hurting jellyfish that are beached on the sand. I have had a save the beach poster made into postcards on sale at Sea Life with the money being donated to them.

I wanted to make this book to teach everyone that they should look after our planet by upcycling and recycling items. Also to teach people how we need to help the planet and stop climate change. I think if one person reads this and it makes them upcycle recycling then I have achieved something.

I hope that this will then become a series of books to show how different places are being affected and what can be done to help them.

I will be donating 10% of the sale off this book to Caudwell Children. They help children who need autism assessments and have helped me.

I hope you enjoy reading it.

Sun —

Boo

House

Boo

Hello, I am Boo the dog.

I like to go on adventures and find out why we should help the planet.

Why don't you come and join me? I am going to learn about how we can upcycle recycling items.

Sun

Owner

Recycling Bin

Boo

Boo and her owner go into the garden to put the recycling into the recycling bin.

Boo's owner says "look at all these items we have to put in the bin. I wonder what people can do with it instead of recycling them."

Boo says "I have some ideas for how people can upcycle recycled items."

Boo's owner says "that is great we can put them in this book as they are fun to make and can help to reuse the items." Boo then explains that some of the ideas will help the creatures and the planet.

Hanging plant plastic cup basket

What you need:
Plastic cup
String
Permanent markers
Soil
Plant
Scissors

Step 1 – Get the plastic cup

Step 2 – Get the permanent markers

Step 3 – Colour on the outside of the cup however you want

Step 4 – Ask a grown up to put a hole in the bottom of cup

Step 5 – Tie the string around the cup

Step 6 – Tie 2 pieces of string to the string already on the cup to make handles

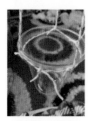

Step 7 – Put some soil in the cup

Step 8 – Put the plant in the cup

Step 9 – Water the plant

Step 10 – Hang it up

Hanging light plastic cup

What you need
Plastic cup
String
Permanent markers
Battery tea light or battery string lights
Scissors

Step 1 – Get the plastic cup

Step 2 – Get the permanent markers

Step 3 – Colour on the outside of the cup however you want

Step 4 – Tie the string around the cup

Step 5 – Tie 2 pieces of string to the string already on the cup to make handles

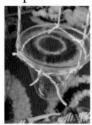

Step 6 – Put in the tea light or the string lights

Tin plant pots

What you need
Tin
Paint
Varnish
Soil
Plant

Step 1 – Get the tin

Step 2 – Get the paint

Step 3 – Paint on the outside of the tin however you want

Step 4 – Varnish the tin once the paint is dry

Step 5 – Ask a grown up to put a hole in the bottom of tin

Step 6 – Put some soil in the tin

Step 7 – Put a plant in the tin

Step 8 – Water the plant

Plastic bottle plant pot

What you need
Plastic bottle
Permanent markers
Soil
Plant
Scissors

Step 1 – Get the plastic bottle

Step 2 – Get the permanent markers

Step 3 – Colour on the outside of the bottle however you want

Step 4 – Ask a grown up to cut the bottle in half (the top part of bottle can be kept to make bottle windsock)

Step 5 – Ask a grown up to put a hole in the bottom of the bottle pot.

Step 6 – Put some soil in the bottle pot

Step 8 – Put a plant in the bottle pot

Step 9 – Water the plant

Plastic bottle windsock

What you need
Plastic bottle
Permanent markers
Pencil
Scissors

Step 1 – Get the plastic bottle

Step 2 – Get the permanent markers

Step 3 – Colour on the outside of the bottle however you want

Step 4 – Ask a grown up to cut the bottle removing the bottom of the bottle is taken off (the bottom of the bottle and bottle top can be used to make flowers or a bee water station)

Step 5 – Ask a grown up to start at the bottom of the bottle and cut around in a spiral to the top

Step 6 – Attach a string around the top

Step 7 – Hang it up

Plastic bottle flowers

What you need
Plastic bottle
Permanent markers
Scissors
Glue

Step 1 – Get the plastic bottle

Step 2 – Get the permanent markers

Step 3 – Colour on the outside of the bottle however you want

Step 4 – Ask a grown up to cut the bottle removing the bottom of the bottle (the rest of the bottle can be used to make a plastic bottle windsock)

Step 5 – Colour the rest of the bottom of the bottle however you want

Step 6 – Glue bottle top to the middle of the bottom of the bottle (optional if you do not want to use the bottle top then you can just colour the middle in)

Plastic bag windsock

What you need
Plastic bottle
Scissors
Plastic bag
Hole punch
String

Step 1 – Get the plastic bottle

Step 2 – Ask a grown up to cut a round strip from the bottle (the rest of the bottle can be used to make bottle windsocks and bottle flowers)

Step 3 – Get the shopping bag

Step 4 – Ask a grown up to help you cut the bag into strips

Step 5 – Use a hole punch to put two holes on each side of the plastic hoop

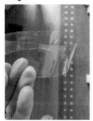

Step 6 – Attach the string to each side to make hanger

Step 7 – One by one tie a strip round the plastic hoop until it is full

Plastic bottle bee sugar water station

What you need
Plastic bottle
Permanent markers
Scissors
Glue
White granulated sugar
Water

Step 1 – Get the plastic bottle

Step 2 – Get the permanent markers

Step 3 – Colour on the outside of the bottle however you want

Step 4 – Ask a grown up to cut the bottle removing the bottom of the bottle (the rest of the bottle can be used to make a plastic bottle windsock)

Step 5 – Colour the rest of the bottom of the bottle however you want

Step 6 – Glue the bottle top to the middle of the inside of the bottom of the bottle

Step 7 – Mix two tablespoons of white granulated sugar with one table spoon of water and put in the bottle top

Tin pencil pots

What you need
Tin
Paint
Pencils
Scissors

Step 1 – Get the tin

Step 2 – Get the paint

Step 3 – Paint on the outside of the tin however you want

Step 4 – Once dry put your pencils in the tin

Plastic bottle pencil pot

What you need
Plastic bottle
Permanent markers
Scissors
Pencils

Step 1 – Get the plastic bottle

Step 2 – Get the permanent markers

Step 3 – Colour on the outside of the bottle however you want

Step 4 – Ask a grown up to cut the bottle in half (the top part of bottle can be kept to make a bottle windsock)

Step 5 – Put your pencils in the pot

Plastic bag upcycling ideas

Toy rocket

Games e.g. bowling

Bug house

Bird feeder

Self water seed station

fairy house

Water can

Decorate it up to use as water bottle

Bird house

Cardboard box upcycling ideas

Decorate them to make storage boxes

Decorate to make them into a recycling bin

Toys dollhouse

Tent

Toy boat

Toy rocket

Toy car

Maze game

Jewellery box

Gift box

Tins upcycling ideas

Wind chimes

Tea light holder

Lanterns

Candle holder

Candle

Cutlery holder

Toy Drums

Games e.g. tin can alley

Yoghurt pot upcycling ideas

Plant seed pots

Flower pots

Basket

Gift container

Pencil holder

Hanging pots

Candle holders

Tea light

Games

Fill with home made yoghurt

Toilet roll tube upcycling ideas

Bird feeders

Toy monsters

Seed starting planter

Toy car

Pencil holder

Paint stencils

Basket

Birdhouse Ornaments

Gift boxes

Phone holder

Egg carton upcycling ideas

Wreath

Seed starters

Grow cress

Toy people

Flowers

Toy monster

Toy boat

Wind charm

Toy caterpillar

Bird feeders

Boo wants to thank you for reading this book. She hopes you enjoying making the items and she looks forward to seeing you on her next adventure.

As well as this book she also has the following books out already for you to join her on her adventures:

The adventures of Boo save the sea animals.

Printed in Great Britain
by Amazon

38314844R00018